MILITARY MACHINES

BOMBERS

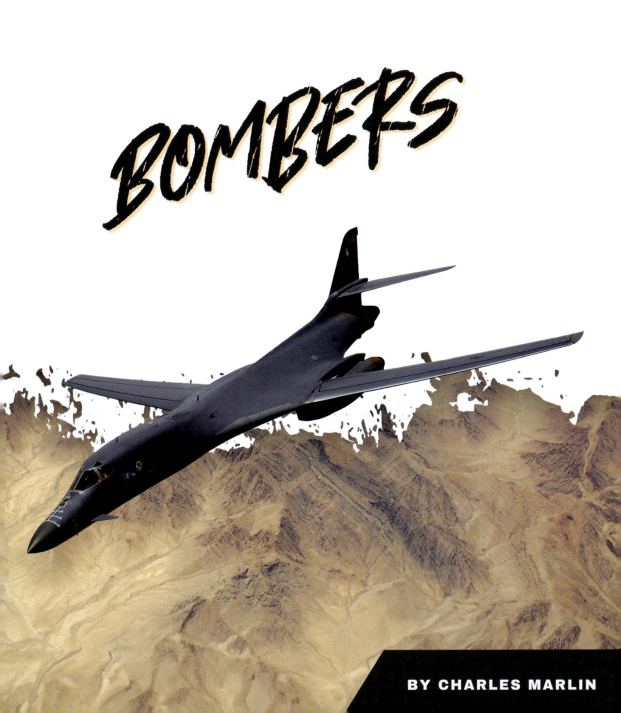

BY CHARLES MARLIN

WWW.APEXEDITIONS.COM

Copyright © 2025 by Apex Editions, Mendota Heights, MN 55120. All rights reserved. No part of this book may be reproduced or utilized in any form or by any means without written permission from the publisher.

Apex is distributed by North Star Editions:
sales@northstareditions.com | 888-417-0195

Produced for Apex by Red Line Editorial.

Photographs ©: Shutterstock Images, cover, 7, 12, 18–19, 20–21, 29; Master Sgt. Andy Dunaway/US Air Force, 1, 14–15, 24; Artem Alexandrovich/Stocktrek Images, Inc./Alamy, 4–5; Staff Sgt. Tristan Truesdell/US Air Force/DVIDS, 6; Mil Image/Alamy, 8–9; NASA/DVIDS, 10–11; US Navy/Interim Archives/Archive Photos/Getty Images, 13; Department of Defense/Defense Logistics Agency, 16–17; Airman 1st Class Jacob Skovo-Lan/US Air Force/AP Images, 22–23; iStockphoto, 25; Tech. Sgt. Alexander W. Riedel/US Air Force/DVIDS, 26–27

Library of Congress Control Number: 2024940124

ISBN
979-8-89250-335-8 (hardcover)
979-8-89250-373-0 (paperback)
979-8-89250-445-4 (ebook pdf)
979-8-89250-411-9 (hosted ebook)

Printed in the United States of America
Mankato, MN
012025

NOTE TO PARENTS AND EDUCATORS

Apex books are designed to build literacy skills in striving readers. Exciting, high-interest content attracts and holds readers' attention. The text is carefully leveled to allow students to achieve success quickly. Additional features, such as bolded glossary words for difficult terms, help build comprehension.

CHAPTER 1
LONG-RANGE ATTACK 4

CHAPTER 2
HISTORY 10

CHAPTER 3
TYPES OF BOMBERS 16

CHAPTER 4
ATTACK AND SUPPORT 22

COMPREHENSION QUESTIONS • 28
GLOSSARY • 30
TO LEARN MORE • 31
ABOUT THE AUTHOR • 31
INDEX • 32

CHAPTER 1

LONG-RANGE ATTACK

A bomber speeds down a runway. Its eight jet engines roar. Soon, the plane flies high over the Atlantic Ocean.

Some bombers can fly nearly 1,400 miles per hour (2,250 km/h).

Tanker planes can carry 200,000 pounds (91,000 kg) of fuel.

RAPID REFILLS

Some bombers can refuel in the air. First, a bomber flies under a tanker plane. The tanker plane lowers a hose or pipe. Fuel flows down. Then the bomber can keep flying.

The bomber flies thousands of miles. Finally, it is over land again. Antiaircraft **missiles** fly at it. The bomber soars higher to avoid getting hit.

Militaries use antiaircraft missiles to shoot down enemy planes.

An MK-84 bomb can cause damage more than 1,180 feet (360 m) from where it explodes.

A few minutes later, the bomber reaches its **target**. It releases many bombs. They fall toward an enemy factory. The building explodes in a huge fireball.

FAST FACT

Some bombers can carry 70,000 pounds (32,000 kg) of bombs and missiles.

CHAPTER 2

History

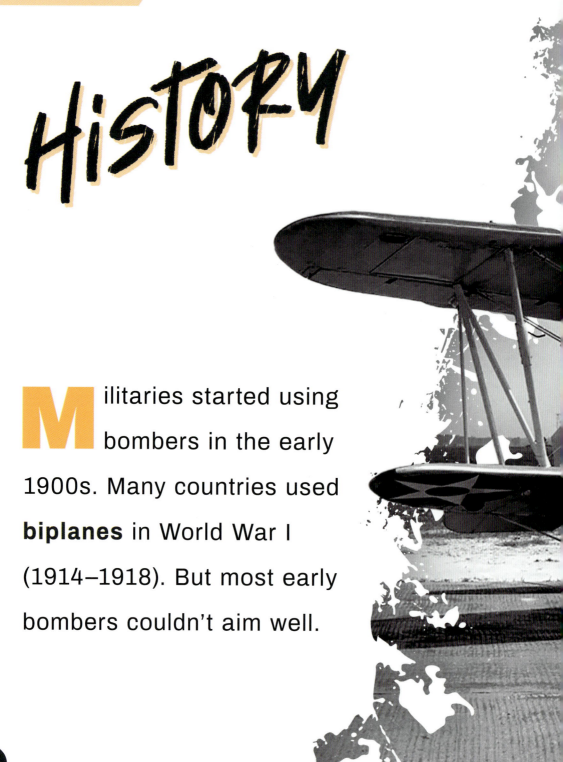

Militaries started using bombers in the early 1900s. Many countries used **biplanes** in World War I (1914–1918). But most early bombers couldn't aim well.

Early bombers were small and lightweight.

Bombers improved during World War II (1939–1945). Heavy bombers carried more **weapons**. Dive-bombers made sharp turns.

Sometimes, hundreds of heavy bombers attacked an area at once. They ruined entire cities.

Germany used Stuka dive-bombers during World War II.

DIVE-BOMBERS

Dive-bombers made steep dives. Then, they dropped bombs. Getting close to the ground helped the bombers aim better. Diving also made the planes hard to shoot down.

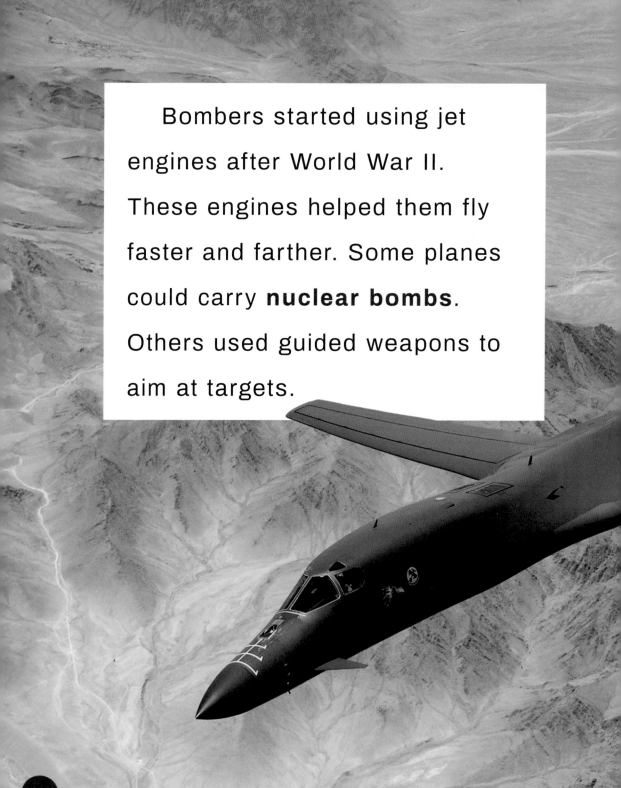

Bombers started using jet engines after World War II. These engines helped them fly faster and farther. Some planes could carry **nuclear bombs**. Others used guided weapons to aim at targets.

The US Air Force has used B-1B Lancers since the 1980s. The large bombers set several world records for speed and range.

FAST FACT

By the mid-1900s, some bombers could fly faster than the speed of sound.

15

CHAPTER 3

Types of Bombers

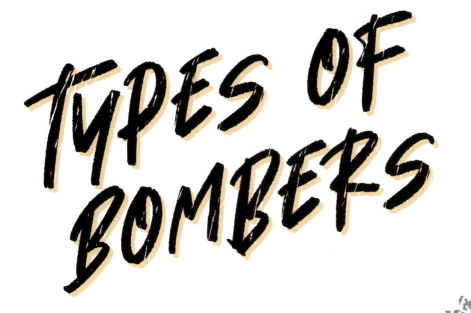

Long-range bombers travel far. Many can fly across oceans. They refuel in midair. Bombers may have more than one pilot. Pilots can take turns sleeping on long flights.

Bombers may fly in a group. They can guard one another from attacks.

Heavy bombers carry many weapons. The B-52 is one example. It can hold more than 100 missiles and bombs.

FAST FACT
The United States has used B-52s since the 1950s.

B-52s can fly 8,800 miles (14,160 km) without refueling.

Other bombers can hide from enemies. They are called stealth bombers. These planes are quiet. They don't leave trails of smoke. And they're designed to not show up on **radar**.

STAYING HIDDEN

Radar finds planes by using radio waves. But stealth bombers have curved edges. This shape stops waves from bouncing back. The planes' paint also takes in the waves.

Aircraft engines are loud. But the B-2 Spirit stealth bomber keeps its engines inside the plane to soften the noise.

CHAPTER 4

ATTACK AND SUPPORT

Militaries use bombers to destroy important places. For example, bombers may attack rail lines or factories. That way, enemies cannot get more supplies.

Militaries may send bombers to attack at night. Darkness helps the planes hide from enemies.

Guided weapons are very accurate. They can hit small targets from far away.

Bombers often help ground troops. The planes fly high above battles. Then, bombers can use guided weapons. They attack enemy soldiers.

FAST FACT
Today, many militaries use drones to drop bombs. These aircraft don't have pilots inside.

The MQ-9 Reaper drone holds several powerful guided missiles.

Pilots aim guided weapons in several ways. Many weapons have cameras. So, pilots can use **remote controls** to aim them. Or people may aim lasers at targets. Guided weapons then follow the lasers.

Most of a plane's tools and instruments are in the cockpit.

SMART BOMBS

Some bombs use **GPS**. Using **satellites**, people find targets on the ground. People send the information to a bomb. Then, the bomb can aim at the enemies.

COMPREHENSION QUESTIONS

Write your answers on a separate piece of paper.

1. Write a few sentences describing the main ideas of Chapter 3.

2. Would you like to fly in a bomber? Why or why not?

3. When did the United States start using B-52 bombers?
   - A. the early 1900s
   - B. the 1950s
   - C. the 2020s

4. What would happen if a stealth bomber left a trail of smoke?
   - A. It would be easier to see the plane.
   - B. It would be harder to see the plane.
   - C. The plane would have to fly more slowly.

5. What does **releases** mean in this book?

*A few minutes later, the bomber reaches its target. It **releases** many bombs. They fall toward an enemy factory.*

- **A.** holds onto
- **B.** lets go of
- **C.** hides

6. What does **improved** mean in this book?

*Bombers **improved** during World War II (1939–1945). Heavy bombers carried more weapons. Dive-bombers made sharp turns.*

- **A.** stayed the same
- **B.** got worse
- **C.** became better

Answer key on page 32.

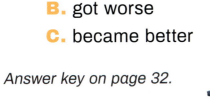

GLOSSARY

biplanes
Planes that have two pairs of wings stacked atop each other.

GPS
A system that uses satellites to figure out locations.

missiles
Objects that are shot or launched as weapons.

nuclear bombs
Weapons that join or split apart tiny bits of matter called atoms to make huge explosions.

radar
A system that sends out radio waves to locate objects.

remote controls
Tools used to guide or direct something from a distance.

satellites
Devices that orbit Earth, often to send or collect information.

target
A person, place, or object that people plan to attack.

weapons
Things that are used to cause harm.

BOOKS

Gaertner, Meg. *US Air Force*. Mendota Heights, MN: Apex Editions, 2023.

McKinney, Donna. *B-2 Stealth Bomber*. Minneapolis: Bellwether Media, 2024.

Vonder Brink, Tracy. *The United States Air Force*. North Mankato, MN: Capstone Press, 2021.

ONLINE RESOURCES

Visit **www.apexeditions.com** to find links and resources related to this title.

ABOUT THE AUTHOR

Charles Marlin is an author, editor, and avid cyclist. He lives in rural Iowa.

INDEX

A
Atlantic Ocean, 4

B
B-52s, 18
bombs, 9, 13–14, 18, 25, 27

D
dive-bombers, 12–13
drones, 25

E
enemies, 9, 20, 22, 24, 27

G
guided weapons, 14, 24, 26

H
heavy bombers, 12, 18

L
long-range bombers, 16

M
missiles, 7, 9, 18

N
nuclear bombs, 14

S
stealth bombers, 20

T
targets, 9, 14, 26–27

W
weapons, 12, 14, 18, 24, 26
World War I, 10
World War II, 12, 14

ANSWER KEY:
1. Answers will vary; 2. Answers will vary; 3. B; 4. A; 5. B; 6. C